Today you can find the tools of the First Peoples. They used stone to make tools. The tools can still be seen across Australia.

This tool crushes seeds and plants. It can crush seeds to make flour. These were called grinding stones. These tools were very important to make food to eat.

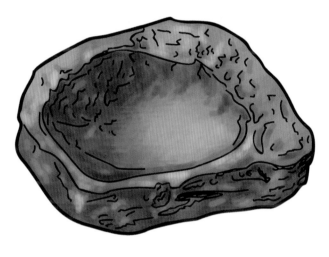

Stone tools could be sharp for cutting. These stone tools are made to be very sharp. This tool could cut animal skins and wood.

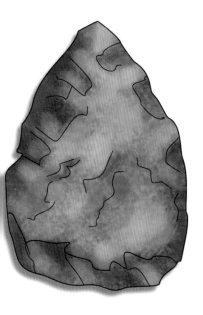  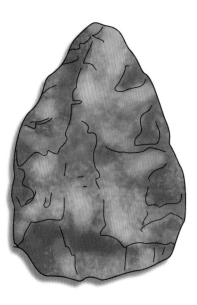

5

Stone tools can be seen lying on the ground in Australia. You are not allowed to remove stone tools. Look but do not remove. The stone tools are to be kept where they were once used.

Stone tools are made from very special rocks. The rocks were taken from special areas. These are called quarries. The First People went back to these areas to get rock which could be made into tools.

9

Stone tools were given handles. This is a sharp stone axe. The axe could be used to chop trees. Axes were used for hunting and digging. The handle was made from a piece of split wood. Twine was used to tie and hold the stone in place.

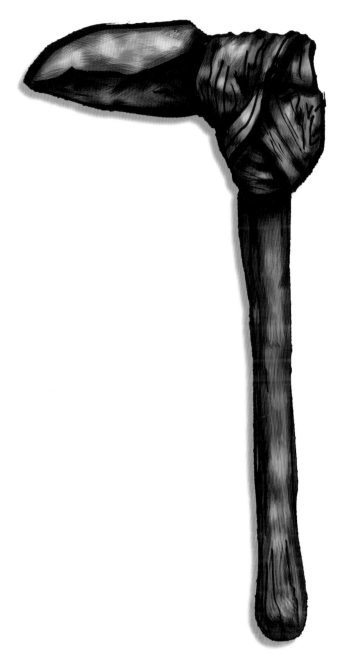

11

Stone tools are found all over Australia. The handles and spears rot away just leaving the stone. The stone tools had different sizes. These tools had many uses as spear heads, scrapers and knives.

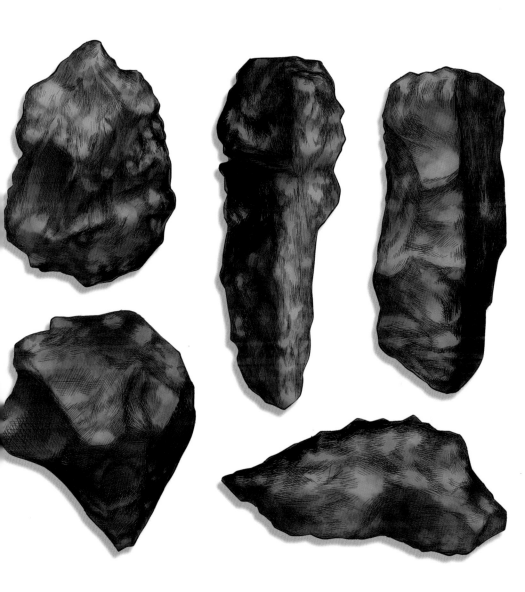

13

Stone tools are made by hitting stone to make sharp sides. The stone would be shaped to make a sharp edge from hitting off flakes of stone. Lots of small flakes could be used for cutting.

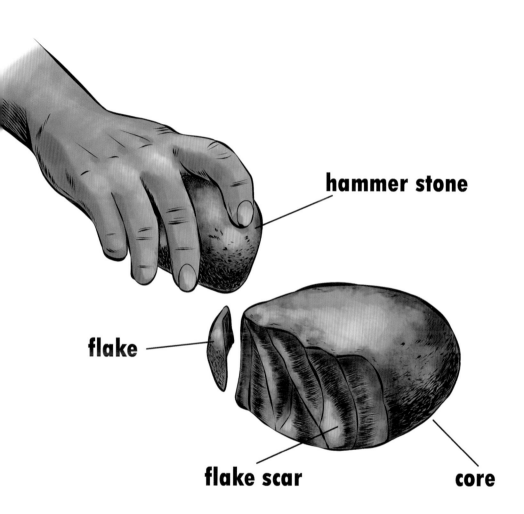

hammer stone

flake

flake scar

core

15

A long knife is made by shaping the sides of a stone. This makes very sharp edges. A handle can be made to hold the knife.

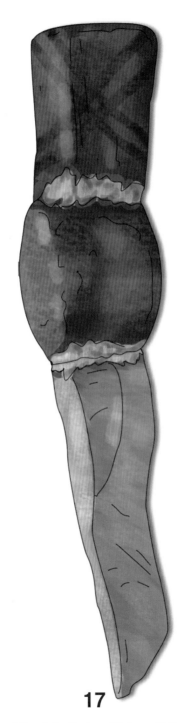

17

These are some stone tools used as spear tips or knives. The spear would be flaked to be sharp on all sides.

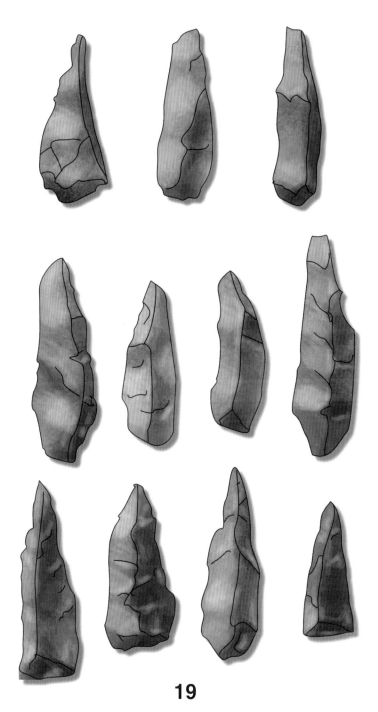

19

The sharp side of the stone tool can be used for many jobs. It can cut and scrape animal skins. It could be made into a stone axe.

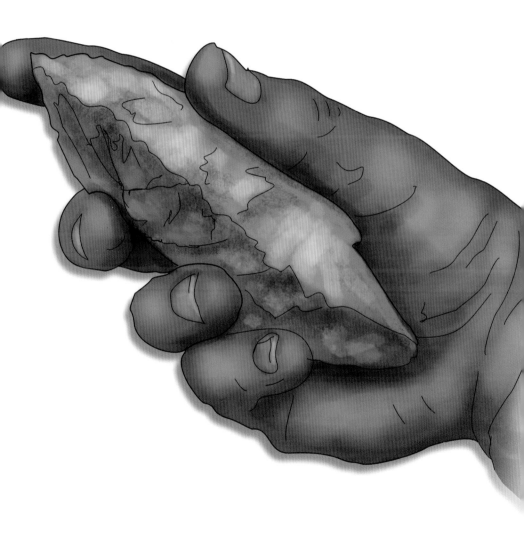

21

In the sides of river beds you may see old stone tools. Study these but leave them for other people to see. Do not remove these stone tools.

22

23

Word bank

stone

crushes

grinding

important

animal

Australia

allowed

once

special

quarries

hunting

digging

split

twine

scrape

flakes